THE DRUMS
SPEAK

———

BY THE SAME AUTHORS

FROM BUSH TO CITY: *A Look at the New Africa*

AFRICAN SUCCESS STORY: *The Ivory Coast*

THE DRUMS SPEAK

*The Story of Kofi,
a Boy of West Africa*

Marc & Evelyne Bernheim

Harcourt Brace Jovanovich, Inc., New York

In West African villages, far from the modern cities, life changes slowly. Kofi's village is at the Ghana-Ivory Coast border. It has a small primary school, but no electricity, and very few adults who can read or write. There you will hear the drums speak. If you stay after the sun goes down, you will find boys listening to the storyteller's legends, for traditions are still kept very much alive by Kofi's people, proud of their African heritage.

With grateful acknowledgment to
Earle Kersh for the layout of the book

From across the lagoon the talking-drum sent out a message, deep into the rain forest. "Gron-don-don!" boomed the tam-tam as Kofi and his uncle Kadjo stopped paddling and listened.

"Kofi, what does the tam-tam say?"

"Something about a meeting, Uncle?"

Kadjo translated the drumbeats into words:

"Clansmen, come home from all your forest camps. A grave matter concerns the chief. He waits till you arrive. Without you he will not decide."

Like a fat orange, the sun still shone through the mangrove roots. Uncle and nephew tied up the canoe and carried their baskets along the narrow path, back to the village. By now women in every compound would be pounding plantains, their pestles hitting the mortars in perfect rhythm: "poom-pedoom, poom-pedoom."

Tonight the village was silent, except for the "gron-don-don" of the talking-drum, still sending its message across the lagoon. Men with storm lamps were hurrying to one another's huts, and in Kofi's compound, his mother and aunts had huddled by the cooking fire.

Kofi's father, Akua, was finishing his supper of yams with red-hot pili-pili sauce. Perhaps now Kofi could ask him about the drum's message? But a boy did not interrupt his elder at a meal. What would the chief say, Kofi kept wondering. Why had he called the clansmen back from the forest? Would there be a warriors' dance this year?

Akua now entered the hut, wrapped himself in a Sunday gown, picked up his wooden stool, and left. Kofi followed his father to the end of the village. He saw him enter the chief's house and waited a while, outside.

"But who is the right one? Tell us!" Kofi overheard his father say.

"Be patient, kinsman. Two moons from now all the men will be back. Then we shall decide." It was the chief who answered. As he tiptoed in, Kofi could see him. But the elder had noticed young Kofi and instantly hushed his voice to a whisper. He looked reproachfully at the boy until Kofi walked out, head very low, for neither women nor children may be present where elders meet.

"Vahee!" wailed the siren of the new sawmill the next morning, so shrill that its sound carried for miles, waking the villages along the lagoon. The sun climbed up the giant breadfruit tree and slowly turned the lagoon from deep purple to pink. A fat lizard shook his sleep-swollen head, and two polka-dotted guinea hens cackled and scratched in the sand for a morning worm.

Kofi's pet monkey, Boubou, ran into the hut, scratched his nails on the straw mat, stuck a wet nose under the blanket, but found himself alone. Kofi was already running to the lagoon to join his friends for the early morning wash.

There was no school today because of the cocoa harvest. Canoes filled with men, boys, baskets, and machetes glided across the lagoon. As Kofi paddled, he started the work song, loud and gay:

> " 'Boys,' the elders said,
> 'Sharpen your knives,
> Paddle across to
> Do our work.
> We are too old to cut cocoa,
> Too old, yo-ho!' "

Kofi's friend Dan answered from another boat:

> "Ahio! Ahioey!
> We the young ones
> Do what they say.
> What else can we do
> But obey? Yo-hey!"

Kofi led his group into the dark forest, opening a path with his shiny new machete blade. Dan followed with the other boys. "Swish-swish, zin-zin, rac-rac" went the boys' blades, glistening in the dark. Kofi had learned to find his way to his father's cocoa grove. He watched for magic charms Akua put up to frighten evil spirits from his path: here a snail shell propped on a bamboo stick, and, farther up, that little bottle with the red parrot feather.

Suddenly, something rustled in the leaves high above.

"He's back!"

The same friendly chimpanzee had surprised them last time. Now he started hopping from branch to branch, challenging the boys to a race. Kofi and Dan ran through the giant ferns, leaped over fallen tree trunks to keep up with him, but when their feet made the dry cocoa leaves crackle, the young chimp shook himself, jumped into the flame tree, and disappeared, cackling at the breathless boys.

Every trip into the forest brought some new adventure. Last Sunday Kofi and Dan had sneaked up on a pangolin that was busy digging up ants with its long, scaly nose. They trapped it. Two weeks ago all the boys had come here and painted their faces with red camwood bark.

Very secretly, where no one could watch them, they had performed the warriors' dance only grown men may do. And in another part of the forest, down by the river, where hippopotamuses wallowed and tall iroko trees grew, Uncle Kadjo, Kofi, and Dan were carving a canoe.

Kofi was happy in the forest, but school meant even more to him. As was the custom of his people, Uncle Kadjo brought him up, and he had always encouraged Kofi in his studies. This was Kofi's last year of primary school. Soon classes would be over and the boys would go to work on their families' farms.

But Kofi wanted to become a teacher. There was no high school in the village, not even in any of the larger villages around. He wished he could go to high school in the city, but it was far away. No boy from this village had ever been there.

Soon after the end of classes, the coming-of-age test would take place. On that day, Kofi and every boy his age was to go to the forest and climb a tall palm tree while the chief and the elders watched. Every boy looked forward to this great event. Those who succeeded would be given greater responsibilities by their elders.

But Kofi was afraid of heights. Every time he got halfway up a tree, he felt dizzy and could climb no farther. His friend Dan tried to help him overcome his fear, but it was no use.

Kofi knew that he would fail the climbing test. He would disgrace himself in front of his family, in front of the chief and the elders. They would laugh at him. All his life they would treat him like a child who could never grow up.

Already Kofi was laughed at. Every time the boys went to practice climbing in the palm grove, they made fun of him, especially Ekra.

"Hey, Kofi-o," Ekra would shout as he swung up and around the tall tree like a squirrel. "Aren't you going to learn, ever? Oh, you're as useless as an empty cocoa pod!"

Dan knew that Ekra's jokes stung Kofi like hot peppers. He would always defend his friend. He would remind Ekra how brave Kofi had been the night of the bush fire, when he broke through the flames to salvage what he could of his father's yam crop. He had even rescued a baby antelope. After that night, no one could call Kofi a coward—not even Ekra. But for Kofi, tree climbing was a different matter.

Akua and Kadjo had arrived at the cocoa grove. This was no time to think of tree climbing. Kofi had to place a basket by each tree. With Kadjo he cut the pods from the trunks and carefully piled them into the baskets.

Something was different this year. At last year's harvest, the men had talked and worried about many things—about the rains that could prevent the cocoa beans from drying, about the wind that could snap slender branches off the young trees. Cocoa was something men always worried about. It had brought wealth to their people for over a century.

This year the men were silent. It was obvious they did not have their minds on their work, and when the baskets were half full, Akua and Kadjo let the boys finish up and walked away to join the other men who sat by the farthest row of cocoa trees, talking and passing around the palm-wine jug.

"They must be discussing the meeting," Dan told Kofi. "Did your father tell you anything?"

Kofi shook his head and went on cutting cocoa pods till all the baskets were filled.

By midafternoon Akua and Kadjo clapped together sticks to give the departing signal and paddled back to the village ahead of the boys.

As the boys loaded their canoes with cocoa pods, something rustled in the mangrove roots. It hissed—it swished in the sand.

"Crocodiles!" Ekra screamed. Terrified, the boys ran back to the forest as fast as they could.

But Kofi neither ran nor panicked. He jumped into the canoe and shoved off with his paddle.

As Dan paddled home, Kofi started opening cocoa pods in the canoe. Back in the compound, Boubou jumped on Kofi's lap, waiting. Inside each pod, wrapping the cocoa beans, was a candy-like flesh. When Kofi opened a pod, Boubou grabbed it, swallowed all he could, and stored the rest in his cheeks.

Now Boubou discovered a mirror in the sand. "Ohi! Ohi!" he squeaked to the monkey in the mirror. He stretched up on his toes, crouched down to look. Was his new friend still there? Yes, but how could he touch him? Boubou swung left, then right. He reached behind the mirror. Nothing happened. He turned the mirror upside down. Still nothing. He licked the image, and suddenly he let the mirror go. The other lips were cold and slippery-smooth. He hopped back to Kofi's lap, closed his sad brown eyes, and went to sleep.

Next morning Kofi unwrapped the moist cocoa beans that had fermented in bags all night and spread them out on racks so they would dry in the sun. Then he changed into his school clothes, took his little sister Yaba by the hand, and joined his friends on the way to school.

All the boys were talking at once. Last night one boy had overheard the principal say to the chief that, for the first time, a boy from this group of villages would have a chance to go to high school in the city. The top students in the final year would soon take an entrance exam. The one with the highest marks would be admitted.

Who would be picked to take the exam, the boys wondered. Who would get the top marks? And what was the city like?

Kofi kept quiet. He hoped the principal would ask him to take the exam. But then—would his father approve?

Kofi did not know it, but last night Uncle Kadjo had already told Akua that the principal wanted Kofi to take the exam. When Akua had objected, Kadjo lost his patience. He spoke about the principal's village that had sent its brightest boys to the city school years ago and, as a result, had six educated men in Parliament today.

"Akua, don't you see?" Kadjo insisted. "This is our chance. You've got to let Kofi have more than just a village education!"

At last Akua told Kadjo why he did not want Kofi to leave.

"If you let him go, I'm afraid Kofi will not want to return to us. Besides, you know what they say about the city: boys get themselves into trouble and are ashamed to come home. Remember the old proverb? 'The young antelope that loses her path ends up lining the drum with her skin.' Kofi's place is in his village."

Though Kadjo alone was responsible for his nephew's future, he would not go against Akua's wishes without consulting the chief and the elders. Most of them had grandsons in school. Some sided with Akua. They, too, feared that if a boy went to the city, he might not want to return.

But the chief had decided otherwise: Kofi must take the exam, he told Kadjo. He would convince Akua himself, but under one condition. If Kofi was admitted to the city school, Kadjo must teach his nephew the traditions before he left for the city.

Now that the chief backed him and his father had been convinced, Kofi made a special effort. Every night he sat in the compound studying for the exam. Tonight it was almost impossible to concentrate. His aunts had gathered by the storm lamp and were gossiping as they braided one another's hair. His sister was plucking chickens, singing an endless ballad, in her steamy kitchen hut. And Boubou was giving lonely little cries, calling for Kofi's attention.

The next morning all his books were put away and the storm lamp went back to the women's cooking corner. Kofi and six other boys went by bus to a larger village to take the exam.

When Kofi returned, Dan was waiting for him at the bus stop. "How did it go?" Dan asked. "Was it hard?"

Kofi seemed hesitant. He told Dan that all the other boys had finished before he had, that he sat alone in the classroom, still trying to figure out the best answers to the last questions.

School was over. On market days, Kofi could now accompany his little sisters and his mother to market in the next village. In the afternoons, he could go fishing with Boubou and the boys. They were all waiting for the results of the exam to come in.

Uncle Kadjo, Kofi, and Dan continued to carve a canoe in the forest. Together they hollowed out the trunk, bit by bit, with hoes, axes and machetes. It had to be perfectly round and as smooth as a mirror. They worked for many hot days, bitten by mosquitoes and stung by the red ants, until it was finished.

As the canoe took shape, Kofi saw what made his people strong:
only when uncle, nephew, and father worked together could the
fields be cleared, the cocoa cut, and the yams sowed. One man
alone in this huge forest could do nothing.

A bottle of rum had to be offered to the water-spirits when-
ever a new canoe was launched. All week, Kofi and Dan had
trapped crayfish. On Sunday, Kofi sold them at the market.
With this money, he went with Kadjo to buy the rum.

All the elders had assembled at the water's edge to watch the new canoe being hauled out of the forest. Kofi gave the rum to Solomon, the storyteller. He would dedicate the canoe.

"Earth and heaven above—" The elder lifted the rum glass and poured the first drops into the canoe. "Let me launch this canoe carved by Kadjo, Kofi, and Dan out of the great iroko tree. Let their journeys be peaceful. Do not tilt them when a crocodile is near, but carry them gently from shore to shore and let them ride as far as the ocean if they must. Water-spirits, grant us this wish!"

Now the elder turned to Kofi.

"The chief has asked me to bring you this news: son of Akua, you will be the first boy of this group of villages to go to the city high school. You have just been accepted."

Everyone drank to Kofi's success, for he had brought great honor to his village. His one great wish had been granted, but Kofi kept his eyes to the ground. The same elders who now drank to him and praised him so highly would soon be laughing at him, he thought, on the day of the climbing test.

With school over, Kofi helped his father on the pineapple farm. In the afternoons Kadjo taught Kofi his ancestors' traditions, just as the chief had asked.

Before teaching him to play the tam-tam, Kadjo wanted to test how much drum language Kofi already knew. He placed his short message-drums by the high bank overlooking the lagoon and sent Kofi down to the canoes.

"Tindin! Tindin!" ordered the drums. "Go on a journey! Push off! Go! Sit down in the canoe! Full turn now!" Kadjo played these commands in short, loud drumbeats. So far Kofi followed the drums' instructions.

"Kung-kekung-keng-koné!" spoke the drum.

But now Kadjo had to stop, for Kofi had misunderstood.

From Kadjo and from Joseph, his other uncle, Kofi learned the fine art of drumming. First he learned simple sounds, then how to call friends, how to play riddles and jokes, how to speak like every animal in the forest.

"Miniki-manaka, that's how the snake wiggles. And the turtledove, how does it go? Koukouhoo-o-hoo!" Every jungle noise had its own beat on the tam-tam, and a good drummer could play it.

One day, as they practiced, Kadjo told Kofi: "When I was your age, the drum used to be our village radio. A good drummer can say anything he wants. Now, let me hear your tam-tam really speak, let me hear it sing so its beat will send the saddest elder dancing down the forest path. Make it ring so sweetly that even the crocodiles will weep for joy."

Kofi learned fast at every drumming lesson. He even made up his own drum sounds. Kadjo was encouraged. Yes, he felt, the chief would be pleased, for this was something Kofi would remember, even in the city.

One night, Kadjo took Kofi to Solomon, the storyteller. From him Kofi would learn the old legends. Tonight Solomon would tell him and the other boys why uncles bring up their nephews.

"Open the palm-wine jug, Kofi. Give me a swallow to clear my throat."

Instantly the boys stopped their chatter and waited for the magic words that would begin tonight's tale.

"When we still hunted elephants," old Solomon began, "your great-great-grandfathers lived peacefully in another land. One day fierce warriors streamed in on them like raindrops from the sky. Our ancestors had to flee through the forest without resting. But they found a river, so turbulent they could not cross. What would happen to them now? The sorcerer spoke:

"'This river will let you cross only if you give it your most precious possession.' Men and women started throwing their bracelets of ivory and heavy gold into the waters, but the river still growled. Now the sorcerer pointed to the king's son:

"'*He* is our most precious possession!' But the queen would not sacrifice her child. The king's sister, Pokou, pressed her son to her heart, lifted him high above her head, and threw him into the howling waters.

"Suddenly one hippo surfaced, and then a hundred more appeared. They formed a bridge for the fleeing tribesmen to cross. Then the hippos disappeared. The enemy was stranded on the other side. Our people were safe.

"Pokou found the king kneeling in front of her to acknowledge her great sacrifice. Publicly the king declared that Pokou's second child—his nephew—would inherit the throne instead of his own son. The king himself would bring him up. And ever since that fateful day, nephews are brought up by their uncles."

The day came when Kofi was to meet the other boys in the palm grove for the climbing test.

"Palms, tall palms,
No one among us is afraid!"

He could hear the boys singing as he walked with Dan and Kadjo to the grove. The chief and the elders were waiting for them.

How many nights had Dan tried to prepare his friend, and in this very spot. But today, Kofi thought, every tree seemed taller, even more frightening.

"Chowe-chowe-chowe!" Five trees away the elders cheered a boy who had just passed his test. Now it was Kofi's turn, and the chief came over to watch with the elders.

Dan helped Kofi get the first solid grip of the trunk. Then he had to let him go.

Painfully Kofi hoisted himself up, just a few inches.

Most other boys would have headed straight for the top branch, cut a coconut, and brought it down without letting it fall, without falling themselves.

"Heels, Kofi!" Dan shouted.

Kofi dug his heels into the notches of the bark and used them for support. Why had the chief picked that one tree? It was the tallest in the grove. The coconuts were unreachable. And up there, Kofi knew there could be vicious little snakes hiding behind the coconut bundles. He knew about the red ants that would prick the skin.

One boy laughed.

"Ekra!" Kofi mumbled. He slipped.

"Don't look down now. Get up there, Kofi! Show him!" Dan shouted.

"You're a fool, Dan. He'll never make it!" Ekra exclaimed.

But Kofi had to look down, though he was scared of heights. He could see Ekra leaving with some of the elders. The chief was still there, but he looked away and so did Kadjo. None of them could bear to see Kofi fall.

Then Kofi saw Dan—the only one who still believed in him, the only one who looked up at him, full of hope.

Kofi clutched the tree tighter. He dug his toes and heels fiercely into the bark. He hoisted himself a few inches higher. "You're a fool, Dan!" Ekra's words kept ringing in his ears. How could Ekra hurt his best friend, insult him in front of the chief?

"If I fail you now," Kofi thought, "you'll never believe in me again!"

Red ants pricked his legs. Kofi did not feel them. He hoisted himself higher, still higher, quite close now to the branch at the very top. He grabbed it, but could not balance himself. The machete was in the way. Thorns were digging into his skin.

With one stroke of the machete, he cut off the coconut. Now he had to get off the thick branch and back to the trunk. He still could not balance himself. The knife dropped. He clenched the coconut stem between his teeth, hoisted himself out of the shaking branch, back to the trunk and down, eyes closed all the way till his foot touched firm ground.

"Victory-victory-victory!" Dan, Kadjo, and the chief shouted. Kadjo lifted Kofi high up on his shoulders. The chief reached for Kofi's hand and took him back to the village in his own canoe.

It was time to celebrate: all the villagers had assembled at the shore to watch the boys' canoe race. They paddled very slowly, very steadily at first so no canoe would tilt. Then their paddles hit the water, faster, still faster. As Kofi's canoe was about to win, it tilted, toppled, crashed into another and another, till all the canoes filled up with water and capsized.

The next morning girls in yellow satin gowns paraded up and down the village street and shouted a message that would wake the villagers still asleep in their huts:

"All the elders, all of the chief's advisers that the drum called two months ago, have arrived from the forest camps. Last night they met with the chief. Come to his compound. He will announce what was decided last night at the secret meeting."

In Akua's compound, Kofi's mother and aunts were painting V-shaped signs on his sister's face. Tonight there would be a festival.

Kofi and Dan had to push their way through the crowd in the chief's compound. There were many elders they had never seen before.

The chief motioned with his fly whisk.

"Be quiet, men," warned an elder. "The words from our chief's mouth are more precious than a golden charm!"

Slowly and solemnly the chief now rose.

"Clansmen," he spoke. "Do not be alarmed when I tell you that I plan to retire. I called these elders back from the forest so they would help me choose a successor. The men of our village had proposed Kanga, Kwame, or Abraham to take my place. But times have changed: we are one of many peoples in a proud new country. We need someone to protect our rights, someone educated enough to go to the city and speak up for us in Parliament."

Kanga the carver, Kwame the fisherman, and Abraham the carpenter lowered their heads in embarrassment. Everyone knew that they had never been to school.

The chief pointed his fly whisk at Kofi. Some of the villagers looked startled.

"Son of Akua, from the beginning I saw in you a future leader. I spoke of you to the elders in this village. But they were against you. 'How can you propose a boy who will fail the climbing test?' they asked me. And when you were accepted in the city school, they said: 'Even if Kofi becomes the most educated boy of his village, he will never be accepted by our people after disgracing himself in the palm grove.' 'Wait and see,' I told them. I prayed you would not fail me. Yesterday, Kofi, you entered your ancestors' clan with dignity. Truly you were the boy who showed the greatest courage by overcoming your one great fear. Elders, I will stay on as your chief a few more years, till Kofi returns from his studies in the city. Then, Kofi, you will wear this crown and golden sandals, for I have chosen you to be my successor. Akua, untie the knot in your heart, friend—your son will return!"